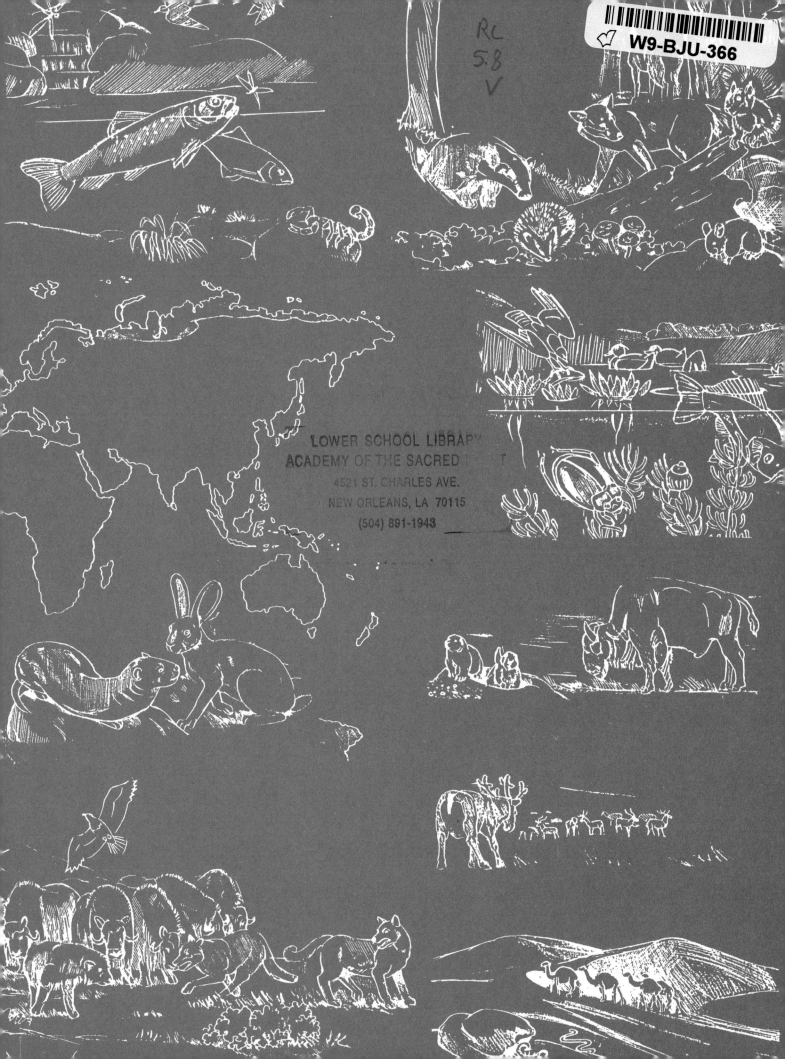

# PLANET
# EARTH

Author:

**Kathryn Senior** is a former biomedical research scientist who studied at Cambridge University for a degree and a doctorate in microbiology. After four years in research she joined the world of publishing as an editor of children's science books. She has now been a full-time science writer for 8 years. She is the author of several books, including **Rain forest** in the *Fast Forward* series and **Superbugs and Minibeasts** in the *Checkers* series.

Series Creator:

**David Salariya** was born in Dundee, Scotland, where he studied illustration and printmaking. He has illustrated a wide range of books and has created many new series of books for publishers in the UK and overseas. In 1989 he established the Salariya Book Company. He lives in Brighton with his wife, the illustrator Shirley Willis, and their son.

Additional Artists:

Nick Hewetson
Simon Calder
Lee Peters
Bill Donohoe
Tony Townsend

Editor:

Karen Barker Smith

Editorial Assistant:

Stephanie Cole

Created, designed, and produced by
**THE SALARIYA BOOK COMPANY LTD**
25 Marlborough Place, Brighton BN1 1UB

ISBN 0-531-11879-7 (Lib. Bdg.)
ISBN 0-531-16445-4 (Pbk.)

First American edition 2000 by
Franklin Watts
Grolier Publishing Co., Inc.
Sherman Turnpike
Danbury, CT 06816

Visit Franklin Watts on the Internet at:
http://publishing.grolier.com

A catalog record for this title is available from the Library of Congress.

Repro by Modern Age.

Printed in China

T 58781

# PLANET EARTH

Written by
**KATHRYN SENIOR**

Illustrated by
**DAVE ANTRAM**
and
**CAROLYN SCRACE**

Created and designed by
**DAVID SALARIYA**

**W**

# FRANKLIN WATTS
A Division of Grolier Publishing
NEW YORK • LONDON • HONG KONG • SYDNEY
DANBURY, CONNECTICUT

# Contents

# 20

## Extreme Environments
Life at the poles, in the deserts, and the
mountains – the animals that survive
and thrive in extreme conditions.

# 24

## The Living Earth and Humankind
Life in rivers, lakes, and woodland, and
the human impact of towns and cities.

# 28

## What an Atmosphere
The atmosphere surrounding Earth,
and the weather.

# 30

## Glossary

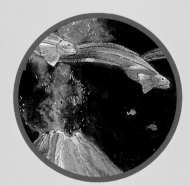

# 31

## Planet Earth Facts

# 32

## Index

# The Big Bang

The universe began with the Big Bang. This is the name given to a huge explosion that happened 15 billion years ago. In a split second, the universe expanded from almost nothing, a tiny dot smaller than a pinprick, into the vast expanse of space. The universe is still expanding — in the billions of years since the Big Bang, galaxies, solar systems, planets, and moons have formed.

Our own planet, Earth, is one of the planets in the solar system that centers on our sun, a star that is part of the Milky Way. The Milky Way is a flat disc of stars that is part of a large galaxy. No one knows how many galaxies there are in the universe.

A galaxy is a group of stars, dust, and gas. The spiral galaxy shown above is one of the most common types. It has coiled arms that spring out from a central nucleus. Elliptical galaxies, which look like flattened spheres, are also common. Irregular galaxies are those in which the stars have not formed into any regular shape. These are the rarest of all galaxies.

# Our Place in the Universe

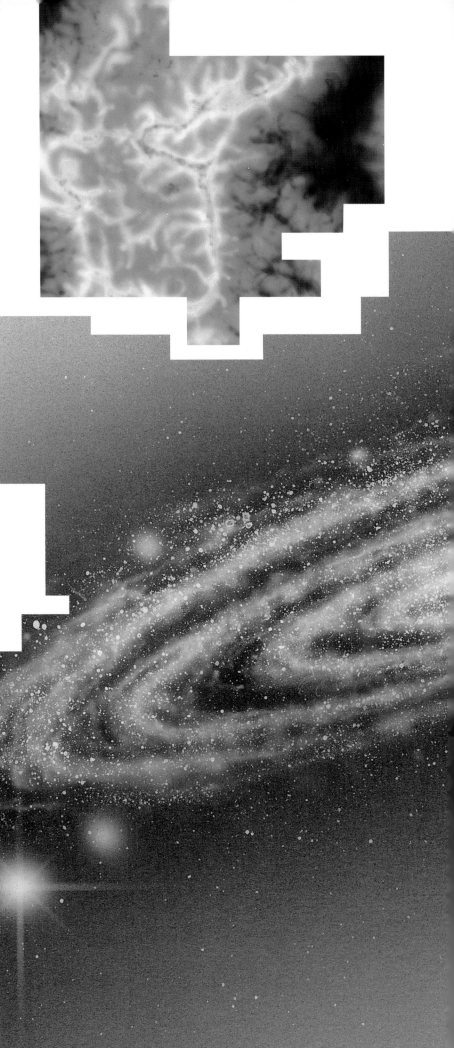

Our own galaxy is a complicated collection of stars, planets, dust, and gas. It is a spiral galaxy that has a central bulge, which contains older stars, and several arms that spin out from it to form a disc. This disc contains younger stars, star clusters, and spiral mini-galaxies, and it is called the Milky Way. Our sun is about two-thirds of the way along one side of it. All the stars that we can see from Earth, at least 100 billion of them, are in the Milky Way. Surrounding the whole galaxy is a spherical halo made up of older stars that group together in irregular lumps called globular clusters.

The sun (below) is the star around which Earth and the other planets in our solar system orbit. It is a shining mass of gas made of 74% hydrogen and 26% helium. In the core of the sun, the process of nuclear fission converts hydrogen to helium, releasing large amounts of energy as heat and radiation.

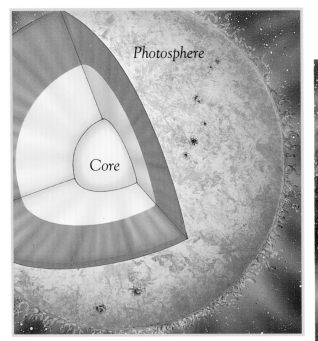

The temperature at the sun's core is incredibly high, and the core is very dense. It is only one-thousandth of the whole sun's volume. The rest of the sun, the photosphere, is mainly gas.

The stars in the universe vary in age, and new stars are constantly forming. Some explode, releasing a mass of expanding gas called a supernova (left). The last supernova seen from Earth was in 1604, but there was also one in 1572, described by the astronomer Tycho Brahe (1546–1601). The supernova, now called Tycho's star, became so bright that it was even visible in daylight. It faded after 18 months but is still detectable as an X-ray and radiowave source.

The Milky Way (above) contains at least 300 billion stars. It has five arms extending from the central bulge. They are called the Cygnus arm, the Centaurus arm, the Sagittarius arm, the Orion arm, and the Perseus arm. The Milky Way belongs to a group of galaxies called the Local Group, which is part of an even larger group of galaxies, the Virgo Supercluster. The Milky Way lies on the outer edge of this supercluster.

8

7

6

5

4

3

2

1

Our solar system consists of nine planets, possibly ten. The inner planets — Mercury, Venus, Earth, and Mars — are mainly rock and metal, and they have no atmosphere, or only a very thin atmosphere. Neither Mercury nor Venus has moons, but Earth has one and Mars has two.

## Our Solar System

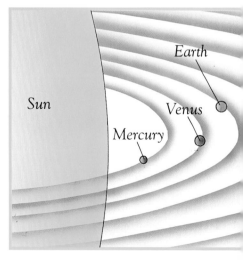

Earth

Sun

Venus

Mercury

10

**Sun**

The sun is at the center of our solar system, and a collection of planets, satellites, comets, dust, and debris orbit it. The planets formed about 4.6 million years ago as debris and matter from space collected together, and balls of gas and dust condensed to form rocky spheres. Many of the planets still show the scars from the impacts of debris. Such collisions were 2,000 times more common 4 million years ago than they are now.

9

## The Planets of Our Solar System (from smallest to largest)

1. Pluto
2. Mercury
3. Mars
4. Venus
5. Earth

6. Neptune
7. Uranus
8. Saturn
9. Jupiter

The outer planets — Jupiter, Saturn, Uranus, and Neptune — all have large numbers of moons (Saturn has 18). These planets have metal cores but are surrounded by huge atmospheres full of swirling gas. Pluto is a very small planet that may have broken off from one of the larger planets. And there may be a tenth planet, but we do not know much about this yet.

Between the planets Mars and Jupiter lies a deep band of rocky debris called the asteroid belt. Today, 3,500 major asteroids have been identified. The largest, Ceres, is over 620 miles (1,000 kilometers) wide. There are also about 100 million smaller asteroids in the belt. Recent asteroids are thought to have formed when a group of minor planets with metal cores and rocky mantles broke up into small fragments.

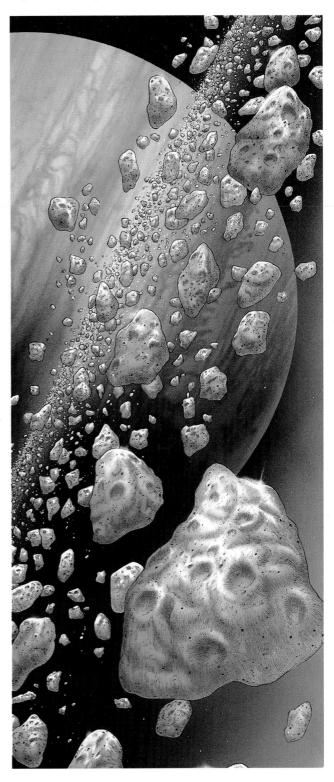

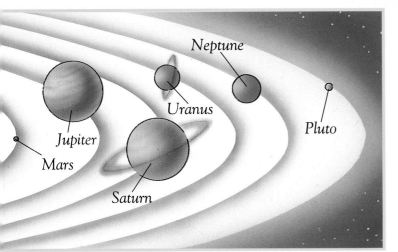

Neptune

Uranus

Pluto

Jupiter

Mars

Saturn

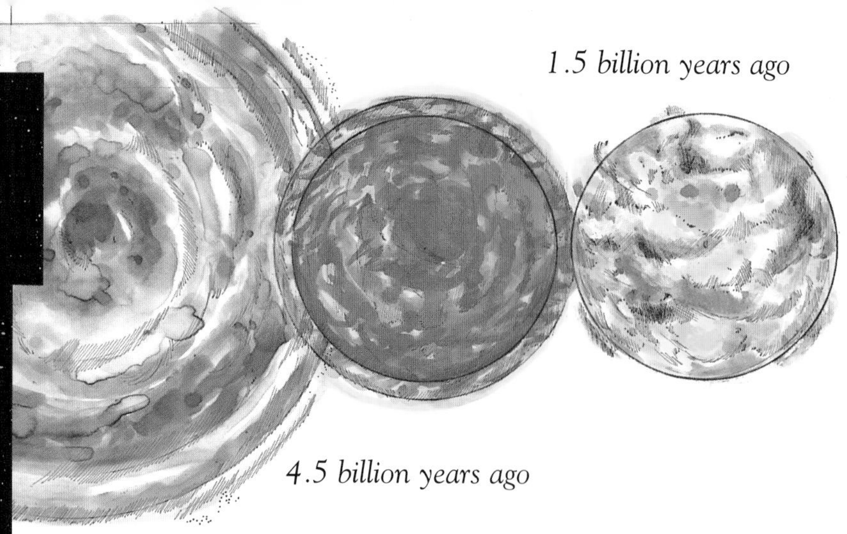

*1.5 billion years ago*

*4.5 billion years ago*

# Planet Earth

E arth is the third planet from the sun in our solar system. It is a slightly flattened sphere that is approximately 7,955 mi (12,800 km) in diameter at the equator. Earth rotates completely once every 24 hours, giving us our day length. It takes 365 and a quarter days to orbit the sun, giving us our year. The extra day is made up in our calendar by adding an extra day to the end of February every four years. Because Earth's axis is tilted at an angle, the amount of heat that gets to the surface of the planet from the sun varies during the year. These variations create the seasons of spring, summer, autumn, and winter.

The moon (pictured above) is the only natural satellite of Earth. Its mass is 1.23% that of Earth, and it has no atmosphere. Its surface is covered with mountains, craters, and plains, which formed when the moon was bombarded with rocks in the past. Radioactive heating in the center of the moon caused some of the surface rock to melt, leaving lava pools that then solidified. These look like lakes, but there is no evidence that running water has ever existed on the moon.

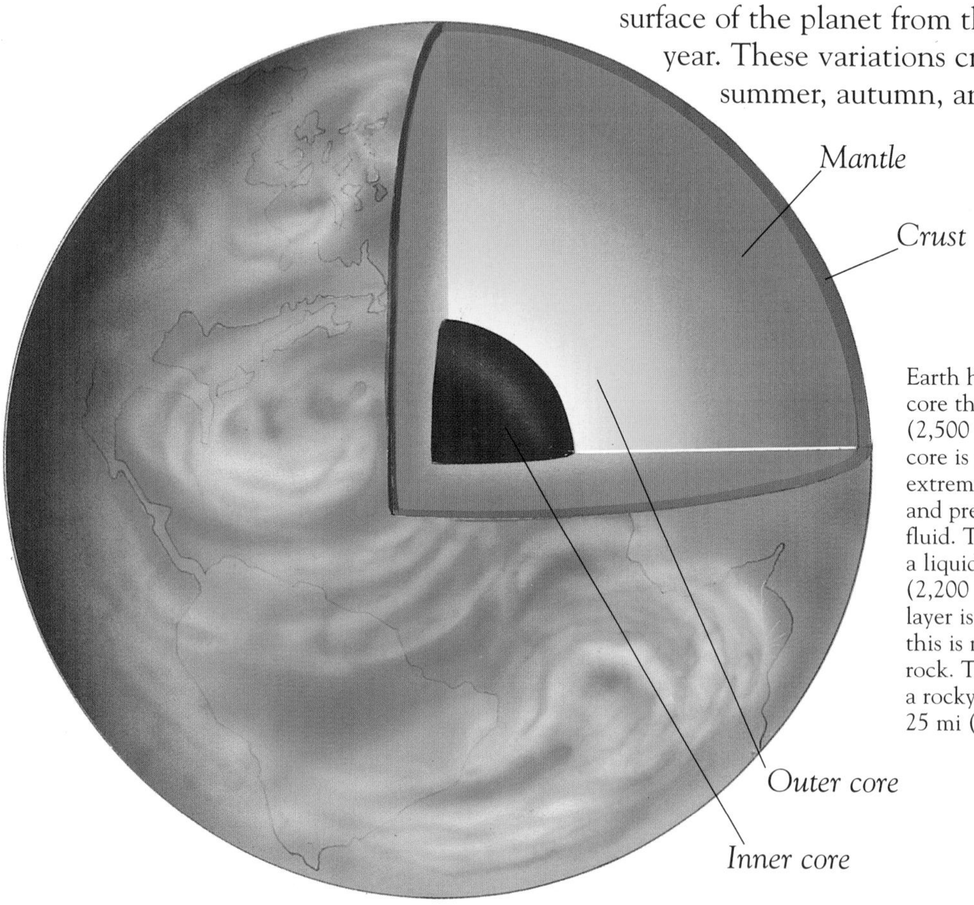

*Mantle*

*Crust*

Earth has a solid metal inner core that is 1,555 mi (2,500 km) in diameter. The core is 90% iron, and the extremely high temperature and pressure keep this metal fluid. The core is surrounded by a liquid outer core 1,367 mi (2,200 km) thick. The next layer is called the mantle, and this is mainly semi-molten rock. The surface is made up of a rocky crust between 3.5 and 25 mi (6 and 40 km) thick.

*Outer core*

*Inner core*

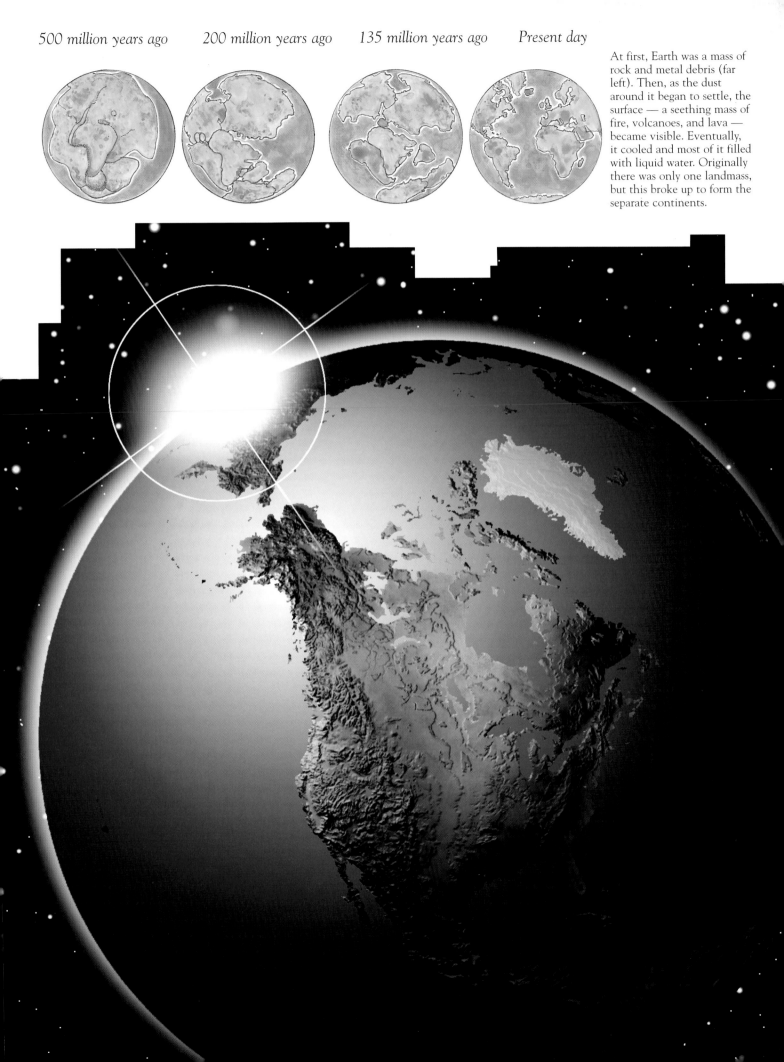

500 million years ago  200 million years ago  135 million years ago  Present day

At first, Earth was a mass of rock and metal debris (far left). Then, as the dust around it began to settle, the surface — a seething mass of fire, volcanoes, and lava — became visible. Eventually, it cooled and most of it filled with liquid water. Originally there was only one landmass, but this broke up to form the separate continents.

Coral reef

1 2 4 16 17 21 20 19 3 5 18 15 6 7 10 9 8 11 13 12 14 23

In the deep ocean abysses, heat vents (right) create pockets of warm water, where bacteria multiply. A variety of creatures have evolved to feed on the bacteria, including the huge giant squid. This creature was thought to be a myth until dead ones were dredged out of the water off the coast of New Zealand in the 1980s.

# Beneath the Oceans

About 71% of the planet's surface is covered by saltwater oceans called the Pacific, the Atlantic, the Indian, the Arctic, and the Southern oceans. The fact that water exists on Earth in its liquid form is one of the main reasons why life evolved here. Without water, nothing can survive. Early life-forms such as bacteria and single-celled organisms evolved in the water, and today the oceans are home to a huge variety of creatures. Rich ecosystems are found all around their shores and near the surface of the oceans. Recently, scientists have discovered that ocean trenches up to 36,000 ft (11,000 m) deep are also bursting with life and are home to many weird and wonderful creatures.

Key to the abyssal zone

1. Rat tails
2. Deep-sea shrimp
3. Deep-sea anglers
4. Stalked crinoids
5. Brotulids
6. Deep-sea eels
7. Gulpers

Abyssal zone

Giant squid

The Great Barrier Reef, off the coast of Australia, is 1,200 mi (1,930 km) long and is the longest coral reef in the world. Crevices in reefs are good hiding places for eels, shrimps, and tubeworms. The trumpetfish's snout is well adapted to searching for food deep within the crevices of the coral. Other animals eat the coral itself: the crown of thorns starfish and the parrotfish can both crunch up the coral polyps.

Hammerhead sharks

## Key to coral reef

1. Green parrotfish
2. Various grunts
3. Elkhorn coral
4. Blacktip reef shark
5. Porkfish grunt
6. Crown of thorns starfish
7. Blue-striped grunts
8. Flamingo tongue
9. Soft coral polyps
10. Young Blue Tang
11. Brittle starfish
12. Tube sponge
13. Sea urchin
14. Sea slug
15. Stinging coral
16. Trumpetfish
17. Soft coral
18. Sea fan lace coral
19. Queen angelfish
20. Queen parrotfish
21. Blue surgeonfish
22. Loggerhead turtle
23. Tubeworms
24. Foureye butterflyfish

# The Creation of Land

The ground that we stand on seems solid, but Earth's crust is an ever changing and dynamic layer. Its surface is made up of large plates that are constantly moving. Where these plates meet, the crust has fault lines along which volcanoes erupt and earthquakes occur. Eight large crustal plates have been identified, but there are also many smaller ones. At the edges of two plates, Earth's surface is very turbulent. The two plates slide past each other, one pushing upward over the other one to form mountains. The other pushes downward to become part of the mantle again. When a volcano erupts, molten rock spews from the top, flowing down the mountain as lava. This solidifies to form new rock.

Sedimentary rocks are formed when particles from dead animals and plants mix with sand in layers on the sea or riverbed (see below). Eventually, the great weight of the upper layers presses down on the lower layers so hard that they turn into rock. Creatures caught in the sediment turn into fossils as the rock forms.

*Asia*

*North America*

*Australia*

*Leaf*

*Shells*

*Mid-oceanic ridge*

*Point where crustal plates meet*

*Fish*

The rock that makes up Earth's crust is constantly being recycled. At the mid-oceanic ridges, in the places where two crustal plates meet, there are mountain ranges that rise to heights of 9,840 ft (3,000 m) and more. In Iceland, these peaks rise above sea level. Molten rock rises up in the spaces in the planet's crust at the mid-oceanic ridges and solidifies as it cools, creating new rock that slowly pushes the plates apart in opposite directions. At the other end of the crustal plate, the rock slides back down into Earth.

*The crustal plates*

Large mountains can occur where two crustal plates have collided and folded up against each other. This creates the high peaks and craggy features of mountain ranges such as the Himalayas, which lie along the junction of crustal plates. Not all mountains are volcanoes, and not all volcanoes are active all the time: Many do not erupt for hundreds of thousands of years.

*Volcano*

*Mountain range*

Volcanoes can occur both on land and underwater where there is a gap in Earth's crust. Molten rock from the mantle flows as lava down the sides of the mountain, and hot gases burst out of the top. When a volcano erupts, there are also earthquakes in the surrounding area. Most of the volcanoes that are active at the moment are in the Ring of Fire, a circle of mountains around the Pacific Ocean. One of the mountains in this ring, Mount Pinatubo in the Philippines, erupted in 1991. Other famous volcano eruptions include Mount Vesuvius in Italy, which buried the town of Pompeii in a cloud of burning gas and ash in AD 79.

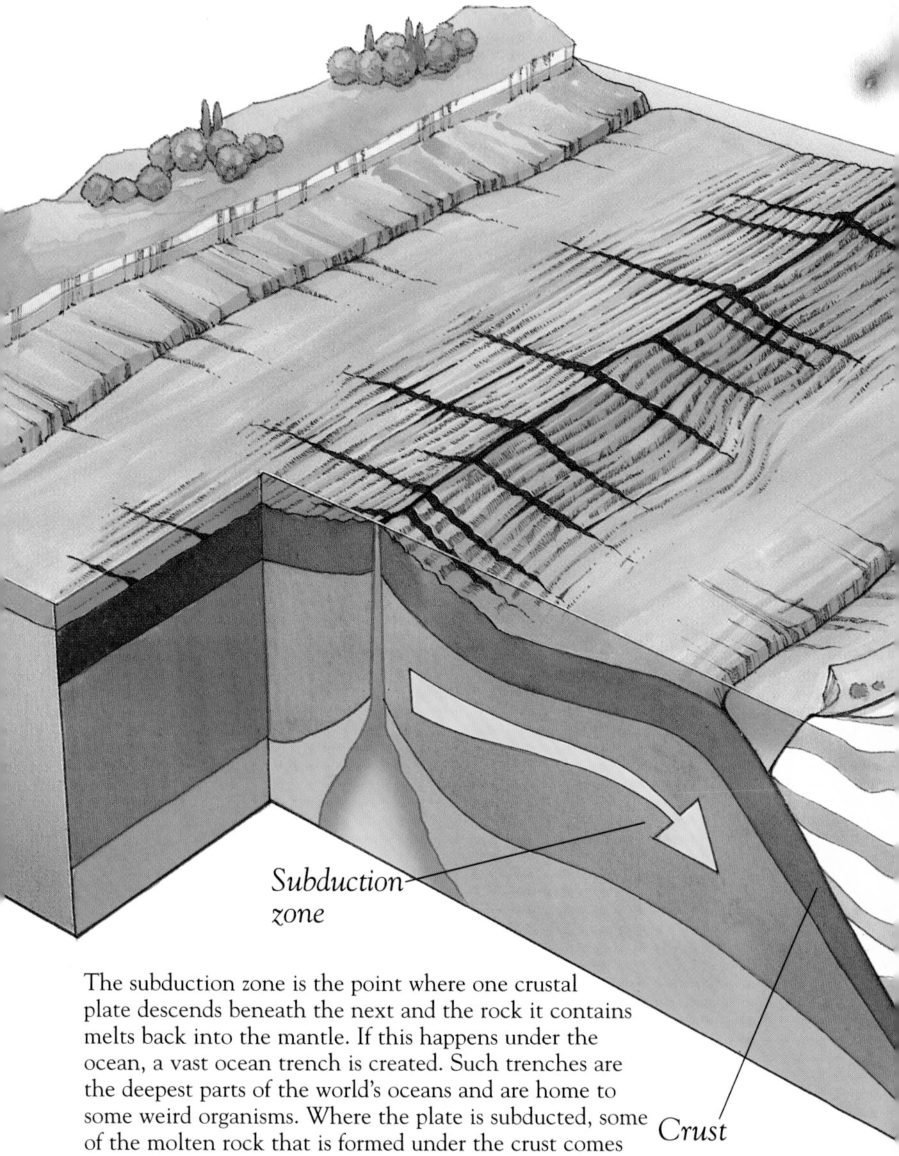

*Subduction zone*

*Crust*

The subduction zone is the point where one crustal plate descends beneath the next and the rock it contains melts back into the mantle. If this happens under the ocean, a vast ocean trench is created. Such trenches are the deepest parts of the world's oceans and are home to some weird organisms. Where the plate is subducted, some of the molten rock that is formed under the crust comes up again, forming volcanoes and mountain ranges. This is how the Andes in South America came to be.

Shield volcanoes (above) have very broad, gentle slopes. They are formed from successive flows of lava that have traveled long distances before cooling and solidifying. Two shield volcanoes, Mauna Loa and Kilauea in Hawaii, both extend over 29,530 ft (9,000 m) from base to peak.

Composite cones, or stratovolcanoes (below), are typical volcanoes, with steep sides and a crater at the top out of which lava and gas erupt. Mount Fujiyama in Japan and Mount Saint Helens in Washington state are both stratovolcanoes.

*Lava*

*Crater*

Mount Fujiyama in Japan (below) is at the junction of three crustal plates. Amazingly, it is not very active, and it last erupted in 1707.

*Molten rock*

# Extreme Environments

The coldest ecosystems on Earth are found at the North Pole and the South Pole. The North Pole is covered by ice all year, and in winter the temperature drops to around -40°F (-40°C). The South Pole is even colder and more inhospitable, with an average temperature of -58°F (-50°C). It is covered by an extremely thick ice cap. Nothing can survive at the center of the polar ice caps, but some animals live at the edges, where it is a little warmer and some plants can grow. Regions of tundra are covered with shrubs, lichens, and mosses, and they also support several types of animal.

*The Arctic*

*North America*

*South America*

*Antarctica*

☐ cold desert

☐ tundra/arctic area

The polar bear's thick fur protects it from the cold. It prefers to eat seals and walrus cubs but will also munch its way through caribou, arctic foxes, birds, and shellfish. Polar bears can live up to 25 years.

Walruses and seals are found in shallow water around the arctic coasts. Penguins are found only in the Southern Hemisphere. Two species, the Emperor penguin and the smaller Adelie penguin, are found in Antarctica.

Reindeer, called caribou in North America, are found in all areas that border the Arctic. Adults stand up to 5 ft (1.5 m) at the shoulder. The reindeer is the only domesticated member of the deer family and is used in Scandinavia for riding and pulling sledges. Reindeer also provide meat and milk. Their hides are used for clothing and shoes, the sinew for thread, and the hair for stuffing mattresses.

In cold deserts there is low rainfall, so only drought-resistant shrubs such as cacti can grow successfully. Reptiles such as chuckwallas bask in the sun during the day, raising their body temperature so they can scurry about and hunt for food. At night, their body temperature falls and they lie still, protected under a rock, until morning.

Scorpions also manage to survive in cold deserts. Like the chuckwallas, their body temperature and activity vary according to the climate. They are formidable hunters because their tails carry enough poison to stun and kill animals many times their own size. They have a thick, waterproof layer on the outside of their body that stops them from drying out in the desert.

Europe

Asia

Africa

Australia

Antarctica

Musk oxen survive the harsh arctic blizzards because of their thick woolly coats and shaggy manes. They are attacked by wolves and used to be hunted by people for food. Their numbers fell dramatically in the early 1900s, but conservation and domestication has now re-introduced the musk ox into the tundra.

21

Cold, dark caves are home to many creatures, some of whom have lost their ability to see. The cave beetle is completely blind, and cave-dwelling bats have very poor eyesight. They rely on sonar signals to find their way about and to locate prey, sending out high-pitched sounds and listening for the echoes. The direction of the echo gives the bat the position of objects.

The Arctic

North America

South America

Antarctica

prairies or steppes

mountains

caves

hot deserts

islands

Climbers such as the ibex manage to survive just below mountain summits and have little competition. Lower down, on the more sheltered slopes, a huge number of animals jostle for space. Grazing animals such as sheep and goats occupy the regions just above the tree line, together with birds of prey like the bald eagle. Farther down, species of bear and deer live alongside smaller mammals such as rabbits and weasels.

Isolated areas of land, particularly islands, are often home to unusual species of animals. The finches found only in the Galápagos Islands gave Charles Darwin his first ideas about the theory of evolution. In Australia, there are animals that have evolved nowhere else, such as kangaroos, koala bears, and wallabies.

Europe

Asia

Africa

Australia

Antarctica

Cold deserts in Patagonia, Turkmenistan, and Gobi have hot summers but bitterly cold winters with some snow. In hot deserts such as Sahara, Kalahari, and Thar, there is no winter; it is hot year-round. The Arabian and Australian deserts quite often have no rain for years.

Away from the two poles, toward the equator, the climate becomes warmer. In areas that also have good rainfall, ecosystems are more hospitable and support a wider variety of life. Features such as islands, mountains, caves, deserts, and flat plains create conditions that often have their own specific climates. Animals and plants living in these types of ecosystems have evolved to cope with the particular conditions there. Most animals and plants are restricted to a few types of ecosystem: a desert-dwelling snake, for example, could not live in the arctic tundra.

Mountains are dramatic features of Earth's landscape, and they provide a huge range of habitats. The tops of the highest mountains are snow-covered, with strong winds and freezing temperatures. The air is thin because of the high altitude, and the soils are thin and rocky, making walking difficult. The highest peaks of mountain ranges such as the Himalayas and the Andes are just as inhospitable as the poles.

The prairies are areas of flat grassland in central North America. Common prairie dwellers are the buffalo and the prairie dog (above).

The steppes are great Russian plains that are cold in winter and warm and dry in summer. The hoofed saiga (below) is the most common hoofed animal on the steppes.

The only animals that can live in hot deserts are those that can go for long periods without water and that can cope with the sharp swings in temperature, such as sand snakes and camels (below).

23

# The Living Earth...

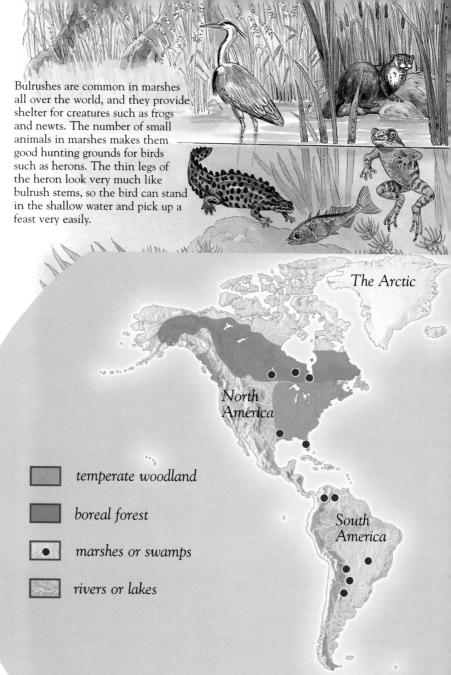

The oceans and seas cover 70% of Earth's surface with saltwater. There are also, however, regions of freshwater within the land — rivers, streams, lakes, and marshes. Rivers begin as small streams of freshwater from a spring, an underground lake, or melting ice on a mountain top. As each stream flows through the land, it joins up with others, and they eventually form a deep river that cuts its way to the sea through soft rock and soil. Some rivers flow into deep depressions in the ground to form lakes. Swamps and marshes are permanently flooded and provide a home for many plants and animals.

Bulrushes are common in marshes all over the world, and they provide shelter for creatures such as frogs and newts. The number of small animals in marshes makes them good hunting grounds for birds such as herons. The thin legs of the heron look very much like bulrush stems, so the bird can stand in the shallow water and pick up a feast very easily.

The Arctic

North America

South America

Antarctica

- ▢ temperate woodland
- ▢ boreal forest
- ▢ marshes or swamps
- ▢ rivers or lakes

The trout (above) is common in rivers across Europe. It likes to eat adult damselflies but has to compete with birds such as swallows, which catch insects flying around close to the river surface.

Trout need fast-flowing water full of oxygen and so are not common in slow-moving lakes. Here, fish such as roach (below) thrive, because they can cope with water of almost any quality. Lakes are also home to larger insects such as the great diving beetle (below left).

The shallow pools revealed as the tide goes out in coastal regions are home to hermit crabs, anemones, common starfish, mussels, limpets, and seaweeds such as bladder wrack.

The force of gravity makes the sea bulge out on the part of the planet nearest the moon. As Earth rotates, different parts of the sea are nearest to the moon, resulting in the tide going in and out twice every day.

Boreal forests are found in the cold regions of northern Europe, Asia, and North America. The trees in boreal forests are evergreen conifers — fir, larch, spruce, and pine. Animals such as wolverines, elks, and lynx also thrive. The wolverine, a large relative of the weasel, is very tough and often competes with wolves and bears for food.

Europe

Asia

Africa

Australia

Antarctica

Temperate woodlands are found mainly in Europe and the east of North America. The trees that grow there are deciduous, such as oak, beech, linden, lime, sycamore, maple, and hickory. Many small mammals such as badgers, foxes, gray squirrels, hedgehogs, and woodmice live in temperate woodland.

About a tenth of the planet's land surface is now cultivated. In the farming regions of western Europe, eastern China, and the midwestern United States, the natural environment has been replaced by fields of grain, fruit, and vegetable crops. In Asia, there are huge areas of flooded paddy fields for rice crops, and throughout the tropical regions there are large plantations of bananas, pineapples, coffee, and tea.

The Arctic

North America

South America

Antarctica

■ tropical rain forest

●  cities

□ cultivated land

■ tropical grassland

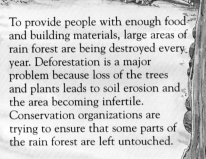

To provide people with enough food and building materials, large areas of rain forest are being destroyed every year. Deforestation is a major problem because loss of the trees and plants leads to soil erosion and the area becoming infertile. Conservation organizations are trying to ensure that some parts of the rain forest are left untouched.

# ...and Humankind

All people come from a small band of African hominids that evolved about 2 million years ago. The world's population has been growing for 10,000 years and in the year 2025 will reach about 8.5 billion people. As the population grows, Earth's natural resources are becoming more scarce. Forests, grassland, and rain forest are exploited, which frequently means the wildlife there loses its home and even becomes extinct. Recently, people have started to understand that we cannot keep doing this; we have to conserve species and protect the rain forests.

Europe

Asia

Africa

Australia

Antarctica

The giant cities of New York, London, Paris, and Moscow extend over hundreds of miles. Buildings of 100 stories or more are not uncommon as housing and office blocks extend upward. Poorer cities such as Delhi and Madras in India suffer from massive overcrowding, disease, and poverty.

Although cities appear to be dominated by people, lots of different types of wildlife manage to make a home there as well. Birds adapt well to a city environment, and foxes and squirrels live quite happily in the center of towns in Europe. Houseflies are also a common feature of every city and town in the world.

Rain forests (above) provide the richest environments on Earth. The most species-rich plot of rain forest is in Peru, where 283 species of trees were found in 2.5 acres (1 hectare).

The variety of plant food means that many different types of animals survive in the rain forest. Macaws, morpho butterflies, and tree frogs are all found there.

The tropical grasslands of Africa are hot flat plains filled with large mammals such as antelopes, gazelles, and zebras. These hoofed animals themselves provide food for the predators of the savannah — the lions, tigers, cheetahs, and hunting dogs. The largest mammals on Earth are also found there, including rhinoceroses, buffalo, and elephants.

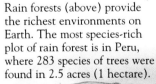

27

The thermosphere is the deepest layer of our atmosphere. It starts at about 54 mi (87 km) above the ground and continues to a height of 310 mi (500 km). The temperature rises from a very chilly -148°F (-100°C) to scorching temperatures over 930°F (500°C). The exosphere is the upper limit of the atmosphere.

The mesosphere lies between 30 and 54 mi (50 and 87 km) above the ground. This is the layer in which rock fragments and debris from space burn up. The temperature falls again through this layer, and at the top of the mesosphere it is barely -148°F (-100°C).

The stratosphere extends from about 6 to 30 mi (10 km to 50 km) above Earth's surface. This is the layer in which airplanes fly. The conditions in the statosphere are relatively stable — there is no weather here. The temperature is constant over the first 6 mi (10 km) and then it rises to about 32°F (0°C) at the border with the mesosphere.

The ozone layer in the stratosphere protects Earth from damaging ultraviolet radiation that comes from the sun. The use of chemicals such as CFCs has caused a hole in the ozone layer over the South Pole that is getting bigger all the time. CFCs and other chemicals that damage the ozone layer are now banned.

The troposphere starts at the ground and ends about 6 mi (10 km) from the surface of the planet. This is where most weather happens. The temperature at the surface is about 68°F (20°C) but at the upper end of the troposphere it is very cold, about -58°F (-50°C).

This curve shows how the temperature changes throughout the atmosphere starting from Earth's surface (the bottom of the chart) and traveling up to the outermost limits of the exosphere (the top of the chart).

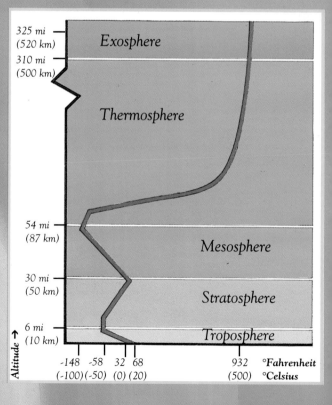

| Altitude → | | | | | | | |
|---|---|---|---|---|---|---|---|
| 325 mi (520 km) | | | Exosphere | | | | |
| 310 mi (500 km) | | | | | | | |
| | | | Thermosphere | | | | |
| 54 mi (87 km) | | | | | | | |
| 30 mi (50 km) | | | | | Mesosphere | | |
| 6 mi (10 km) | | | | | Stratosphere | | |
| | | | | | Troposphere | | |
| | -148 (-100) | -58 (-50) | 32 (0) | 68 (20) | | 932 (500) | °Fahrenheit (°Celsius) |

The thick clouds that form around a hurricane contain fine droplets of water that fall as heavy rain when the hurricane touches the surface of the planet.

The huge circle of clouds around a hurricane can be picked up at quite an early stage by satellite. This allows weather centers around the world to track the hurricane and warn people who are living in its path.

# What an Atmosphere

Earth is surrounded by a layer of gas. This is the atmosphere, and it is divided into several layers. The main layers are the troposphere, the stratosphere, the mesosphere, the thermosphere, and the exosphere. The troposphere is the layer nearest to the surface of the planet. Circulation of air there causes the weather patterns that can change by the hour. Weather is caused by warm and cold air traveling at different speeds, different air pressures, and different amounts of moisture in the troposphere. Distinct weather patterns are found in most parts of the world. In the subtropics, weather is seasonal — long dry periods are followed by a couple of months of wet monsoons. Other parts of the world have more unpredictable weather. Extremes of weather such as hurricanes, tornadoes, cyclones, and droughts are destructive and wreak havoc where they strike.

This diagram (above) shows what happens inside a hurricane. It forms as warm damp air rises and colder air is sucked in to replace it. As in a tornado, the two kinds of air start spiraling, causing a fast swirling wind that travels at high speed, reaching 217 mph (350 kph) in the strongest gusts. Hurricanes are much bigger than tornadoes and can cause a lot more damage over a wider area. They have a column of warm air in the center — called the eye of the storm — around which the swirling winds rotate.

Monsoons (left) happen when a sudden change in wind direction causes clouds laden with water to move over warm land. This happens every year between April and October in India and Bangladesh. The rains can be torrential and can last for weeks, often resulting in flooding and loss of crops.

Tornadoes arise when banks of cold air and warm air meet. A large tornado can be 164 ft (50 m) across and have winds that travel at 155 mph (250 kph).

# Glossary

**Climate**
The weather conditions typical on a particular part of Earth. The Arctic, for example, has a cold climate; tropical rain forests and deserts have hot climates.

**Continent**
A mass of land on Earth. There are seven of them — Asia, Africa, North America, South America, Antarctica, Europe, and Australia.

**Debris**
A mixture of rocks and dust that floats around in space.

**Deciduous**
Plants that lose their leaves in winter and grow new ones in spring.

**Density**
How compact an object is. For example, lead is extremely dense, but wood and materials such as polystyrene that contain lots of air pockets are much less dense.

**Domesticated**
Animals that have been tamed and reared by people. Common examples include cattle, sheep, and pigs.

**Earth's Axis**
This is an imaginary line drawn straight through Earth between the North and South poles. Because the planet is tilted, this line is not vertical; it is at an angle of just less than 24°.

**Ecosystem**
The physical environment and the living organisms that exist at a particular place on Earth. A desert ecosystem, for example, would include sand dunes and the camels and snakes that live on them.

**Equator**
An imaginary line drawn around the center of Earth, where the planet is at its widest.

**Evergreen**
Plants that keep their leaves year-round.

**Evolution**
The process by which animals and plants change and develop over long periods of time. All life evolved from bacteria and single-celled organisms that first appeared on Earth 3.5 billion years ago.

**Habitat**
A place where animals or plants live.

**Heat vent**
A hot spring on the seabed.

**Hemisphere**
A half of Earth. The equator divides the Northern and Southern hemispheres, and a line passing through the North and South poles divides the Eastern and Western hemispheres.

**Hominids**
Ape-like animals that walk upright on two legs. Both early and modern man are hominids.

**Mammal**
A warm-blooded animal that gives birth to live young and feeds them with its own milk. People, lions, and elephants are examples of mammals.

**Mantle**
The layer of molten rock that lies under Earth's crust.

**Meteor**
A piece of rock from space that reaches the outer limits of Earth's atmosphere, where it becomes very hot and bright and usually burns up.

**Orbit**
An object that travels around another object is said to be in orbit. Earth travels in an orbit around the sun.

**Planet**
A spherical (usually) object in space that forms from the gas and dust around a star. It does not produce its own light and can be seen only by the reflected light of a star. In our solar system, there are nine known planets, including planet Earth.

**Polyp**
Sea creatures that look like plants but are actually animals. All polyps have a stage in their life cycle when they attach themselves to a rock or other hard surface under the sea. Examples of polyps are sea anemones, hydras, and corals.

**Predator**
An animal that hunts another animal for food.

**Reptile**
A cold-blooded animal with a backbone and an internal skeleton that tends to have dry, scaly skin. Turtles, lizards, snakes, crocodiles, frogs, and toads are all reptiles.

**Satellite**
An object that orbits a planet. Natural satellites are moons; there are also satellites around Earth that are artificial, such as weather and communications satellites.

**Savannah**
Tropical grasslands.

**Solar System**
The system of nine known planets that orbits our sun.

**Space**
The empty part of the universe that is between the planets, stars, and galaxies. It contains nothing, not even gas.

**Species**
A group of animals that all look and behave the same and that breed together to produce young that are also the same.

**Tundra**
Very cold areas bordering the Arctic and Antarctic regions where only small plants can grow.

**Weather**
The patterns of cold, warmth, wind, rain, and pressure that occur in the troposphere.

# Planet Earth Facts

At the equator, the diameter of Earth is 7,927 mi (12,757 km). At the poles, where the sphere of Earth is slightly flattened, the diameter is 7,900 mi (12,714 km).

If you flew all around the planet along the line of the equator, you would have traveled 24,900 mi (40,075 km).

Planet Earth formed about 4.5 billion years ago; life first appeared 3.5 billion years ago; the dinosaurs died out 65 million years ago, and early man first appeared about 2 million years ago.

Earth is approximately 93 million mi (150 million km) from the sun.

It takes 23.9345 hours for Earth to rotate completely and 365.256 days to orbit the sun once.

In its orbit around the sun, Earth travels at 18.5 mi (29.79 km) per second.

The average surface temperature on Earth, taking into account the hottest days at the equator and the coldest nights at the South Pole, is 59°F (15°C).

Earth is the third planet from the sun in our solar system and is the only planet where life is known to exist.

Most of planet Earth is taken up by the mantle — this accounts for 84% of Earth's total volume.

Earth, including its atmosphere, weighs about 6.6 sextillion tons.

It takes 14 billion years for light to reach Earth from the edge of the known universe.

Our sun is about 27,700 light-years from the center of the Milky Way.

The nearest star to the sun is Proxima Centauri, which is 4.22 light-years away.

Evidence from meteors tells us that the solar system is 4.54 billion years old. It probably took about 25 million years to form from gas and dust.

The hottest place on Earth is Dallol in Ethiopia, where the average temperature is 94°F (34.4°C) in the shade.

Human beings are the only creatures that can survive on every continent in the world.

The largest desert in the world is the Sahara in North Africa, which covers an area of about 3.2 million sq mi (8.4 million sq km).

The driest desert in the world is the Atacama in South America; until 1971, it had not rained there for 400 years.

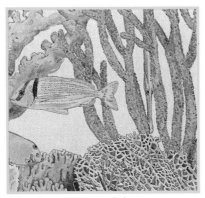

The deepest part of the ocean is the Marianas Trench in the Pacific. The bottom of it is 36,200 ft (11,034 m) below sea level.

The biggest active volcano in the world is Mauna Loa in Hawaii. Since 1832, it has erupted every three and a half years.

The average depth of the seas and oceans is 12,470 ft (3,800 m). If Earth's surface was leveled out completely, it would be covered by 2,460 ft (750 m) of water.

Over 2.5 million different species of living animals are known.

The highest mountain in the world is Mount Everest, which is in the Himalayan mountain range in Asia. It is 29,029 ft (8,848 m) high.

The longest river in the world is the Nile in Egypt. It is 4,160 mi (6,695 km) long.

Ice covers more than one-tenth of Earth's land surface; about three-quarters of all the world's freshwater is frozen in ice sheets and glaciers.

The world's largest freshwater lake is Lake Superior. It covers an area of 31,663 sq mi (82,000 sq km) in the United States and Canada.

# Index